Why should I bother about the planet?

Susan Meredith

Illustrated by Sara Rojo

Designed by Catherine-Anne MacKinnon
and Nancy Leschnikoff

Scientific adviser: Dr Julia Jones, School of the Environment
and Natural Resources, University of Wales, Bangor

Contents

This book was edited by
Jane Chisholm.
Additional advice about the planet from
Dr Margaret Rostron and Dr John Rostron.

What's the problem?

Planet Earth has been around for billions of years. That proves it's pretty tough, so what's the problem?

The trouble is that there are some changes taking place – and they aren't happening naturally and slowly as they did in the past. Most of them are caused by people and the things people do, and they are happening fast.

People have the cleverest brains of any living creature. We've learned how to farm, build cities, create industries and invent aeroplanes. But all this activity is having some unhealthy side effects for the planet and its inhabitants.

So isn't it for governments to sort out the mess? Well, it's governments that have the power to make big changes, it's true, but there's a lot that individuals can do too. In this book, you'll find out what has caused the planet's problems and what needs to be done about them. You'll also get lots of practical ideas for how you can 'go green' and help to save the planet.

Even the smallest actions all add up and can make a difference. And after all, if it's clever human brains that have caused the problems, they are surely bright enough to solve them too.

SAVE

Trashing the planet

Today's problems really started about 200 years ago, at a time known as the Industrial Revolution. People invented machines that could do all kinds of useful jobs, provided they had power to make them work. The inventions were so brilliant that hardly anyone realized there might be a downside.

Energy crisis

To power these new machines, people burned coal, gas and oil. At the time there seemed to be endless supplies of these fuels. But such huge amounts have been used that it's going to get harder and harder to find enough to keep everything going. And burning fuels makes the planet dirty. So we need some new ways of powering our machines.

Litter louts

Modern living creates a lot of different kinds of dirty waste. It comes from power stations, factories, farms, transport, offices, shops and homes. The waste is polluting the air, land and water, and even changing the weather – with dangerous results for living things, including people. We need to clean up our act.

Fewer beluga whales are being born in Canada because their water is poisoned by chemicals from nearby industries.

The clean-up cost

Some people say it will cost too much to make the planet healthy again. It's true it won't be cheap, but tackling the problems now could even save money in the long run. For example, far fewer people would need treatment for asthma if air pollution in the world's cities was cleaned up.

In some cities, air pollution can be so bad that people go out wearing masks.

It's a small world

People in rich, developed countries, such as the USA, UK and Australia, use the most coal, gas and oil, and cause the most pollution. But the damaging effects are felt all over the world, in less developed countries too. Governments need to work together to try to find worldwide solutions.

New lifestyle?

People are starting to rethink the way they live, and the buzz word is sustainability. In a nutshell, a sustainable lifestyle means meeting our own needs without messing up the planet for our children and grandchildren. For instance, plants provide all the oxygen we need to breathe. It makes sense to look after them – not just for their own sake but for future generations.

What energy crisis?

All you have to do is flick a switch and machines spring into action. But our high-tech lifestyles are causing two major problems. Not only are fuel stocks running down, but the fuels are damaging the planet as we use them.

Why are fuel stocks a problem?

Almost all the world's energy comes from coal, gas or oil, extracted from the ground. These are called 'fossil' fuels, because they are made from the rotted remains of prehistoric plants or animals. Fossil fuels have taken millions of years to form and we are using them up at a faster rate than they can possibly be replaced. For this reason, they are also known as non-renewable fuels.

Burning fossil fuels

For the energy in fossil fuels to be released and make machines work, the fuels have to be burned. Power stations burn coal, gas or oil to generate electricity for lights, cookers, computers and hundreds of other appliances. Gas is also burned for heating and cooking. Oil is refined to make petrol and aviation fuel to burn in car and plane engines. But all this burning has some dangerous side effects.

What side effects?

When fossil fuels are burned, waste gases are produced and spewed into the environment. These gases are harmful. Some pollute the air and water, damaging people, animals and plants. Others, such as carbon dioxide (CO_2), are the main cause of one of the planet's biggest problems of all – climate change.

Power stations are a major source of harmful gases, especially CO_2.

What about nuclear power?

Nuclear power, which comes from the metal uranium, can be used to make electricity without producing the waste gases fossil fuels do. But it has a different disadvantage – it produces radioactive waste, which can be lethal to living things and remains dangerous for thousands of years. It is difficult to store it safely and prevent harmful leaks.

Is biofuel a solution?

Some people are enthusiastic about a new type of fuel, biofuel, which can be used to generate electricity or to power cars. It's usually made from crops. But critics say that too much CO_2 is produced while the biofuel is actually being made and transported, and that, in any case, plants should be used to feed people, not machines.

You can find out more about biofuel on page 11.

Hotting up

The start of the 21st century has seen the hottest years since records began. This is evidence, scientists are convinced, that the planet is gradually getting warmer. But why is global warming happening? And why does it matter?

Too much gas

There is more CO_2 in the atmosphere now than there has been for hundreds of thousands of years, and most of the increase has come from burning fossil fuels. But there are other gases that cause global warming too. One is methane, which is given off by belching and farting farm animals, growing rice and rotting rubbish. Another is nitrous oxide, released from farm soil as well as burning fossil fuels. These global warming gases are known as greenhouse gases.

Why greenhouse gases?

When the Sun's rays hit the Earth, most of them bounce away. But there is a kind of blanket of greenhouse gases all around the Earth. The blanket works a bit like a glass greenhouse and traps in most of the Sun's heat. This is vital, as without it we would freeze to death.

The big thaw

There are huge sheets of ice at the North and South Poles, but the warmer temperatures are making them melt. The extra water makes the sea level rise, which means that low-lying islands and places near coasts are at risk of flooding. Some people in the Maldive islands are already having to move, and certain islands may disappear altogether.

Polar icecaps melt.

Sea level rises.

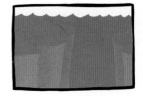
Land is flooded.

Climate change

Global warming means more heatwaves, droughts and floods, but it also means wilder weather in general – more gales and even hurricanes too. Food crops can be ruined by the wrong kind of weather, and diseases that thrive in hot conditions, such as malaria, may spread.

Blanket of greenhouse gases

Heat from Sun

Some heat escapes.

But the problem is that the blanket has now become so thick that it traps in too much heat. This is what's making temperatures rise so dangerously.

Earth

Most heat is trapped.

What's green energy?

There's really no need for us to pump out so many greenhouse gases. There are clean, renewable sources of energy that we could use instead. At the moment, less than 5% of the world's energy comes from clean renewables. We could convert to much, much more of this green, planet-friendly energy.

Solar power

Solar water-heating panels on roofs can be used to capture the Sun's heat energy and warm the water that runs through them. This then goes to the storage tank for your house's hot water and central heating radiators. Even in countries where it's often cloudy, enough sun still gets through to heat a lot of water this way.

Another type of solar panel – photovoltaic (PV) – converts the Sun's rays into electricity, but this needs more sunshine.

Wind power

The power of the wind can also be used to create electricity. The wind turns the blades of a wind turbine, the blades drive generators inside, and these make electricity. Wind turbines work best on hills or out at sea where the wind is strongest. Small turbines on houses in built-up areas are not very effective.

One large wind turbine in a windy place can create enough electricity to power 1,000 homes.

Water power

Some of the world's electricity is produced by hydroelectric power, which uses the power of rushing water to turn turbines. But this needs big dams to store the water and land has to be flooded to build them – not good for the people, animals or plants living there. Now, there are new projects that use the power of ocean tides and waves to create electricity, ideally with less environmental damage.

Sustainable biofuel

Some farmers make biofuel from the harmful methane released by their rotting waste crops, wood or animal poo. They collect the gas in tanks called fermenters, where it is transformed into electricity. So they get rid of rubbish, supply themselves with energy and cut down on global warming all at the same time.

A petrol substitute called bioethanol could also be produced sustainably. The best way might be to make it from wood grown on land that isn't needed for crops.

What green gadgets could I use?

Look out for solar-powered calculators, watches, torches, and even MP3 or mobile phone chargers – great when you are on the move. Most come with batteries that will recharge if you leave the gadget in the sun. Or you could try using your own energy to power a wind-up radio.

How can I save energy?

It's surprising how many ways there are to save energy – painless ones too. What's more, your home's bills will be lower and that'll please your parents.

Switch it off

Every time someone goes out of a room and leaves their TV or light switched on, they're polluting the planet with greenhouse gases, for no reason at all. Help reduce dangerous climate change and save money at the same time by following these tips.

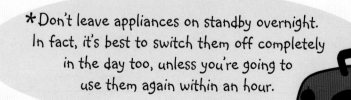

* Switch off appliances when you're not using them. After all, it only takes a second to turn them back on again. This includes TVs, DVD players, hi-fis, and chargers. Chargers carry on using electricity even if you've detached the phone or MP3 player.

* Don't leave appliances on standby overnight. In fact, it's best to switch them off completely in the day too, unless you're going to use them again within an hour.

* Screensavers don't save energy. If you're going to be away from your computer for more than an hour, put it in sleep mode or, even better, shut it down. A computer monitor left on overnight wastes enough energy to microwave six dinners.

* Turn off the lights every time you leave a room.

* Use energy-saving light bulbs. They're expensive to buy but cheaper to run and last 8-12 times longer than ordinary bulbs. If they don't give out a strong enough light to use all over the house, at least put them in places that don't really need to be very bright. In any case, these bulbs are becoming more efficient all the time. If every family in the UK used just three of them, enough energy would be saved to power all the country's street lights.

* If you're cold, make sure you're wearing enough clothes and that the windows are shut, before you put on the heating. Closing your curtains after dark helps keep heat in too.

* If you're hot, turn your radiator down instead of stripping off your jumper. There's usually no need to have a living room heated above 20°C. You can use a room thermometer to check the temperature.

Saving energy in the kitchen

The kitchen is a really high-energy room, so there's a lot of scope for making big savings here.

* Only put as much water in the kettle as you really need, so it will heat up quicker. (Don't be too stingy, though – you need to cover the element so it doesn't boil dry.)

* Don't put too much water in saucepans, and match the size of the pan to the ring. A small pan on a big ring wastes energy and a big pan on a small ring won't cook efficiently. Stacked steamer pans are energy-efficient because you only use one ring. To cook food faster, cut it into smallish chunks and put the pan lid on.

* Don't keep looking in the oven to see if your food is cooked. Heat will escape, so it will end up taking longer.

* Cook more food than you need and freeze some of it for another time. Reheat it in the microwave, as this uses much less energy than a hob or oven.

* Wait until you have a full load before you put the washing machine on, or use the mini-load setting if you have one. A 40°C wash uses a third less energy than one at 60°C, and modern detergents wash well at 40°C, or even 30°C.

* Dry clothes outside or on an airer if you can. Tumble dryers use more energy than any other household appliance.

* Don't put the dishwasher on until it's full, and use the eco-cycle if you have one, unless the dishes are really dirty.

* Don't leave fridge or freezer doors open, even for a minute, because they have to use extra energy to cool the temperature back down again. The same thing happens if you put hot leftovers in the fridge. Let the food cool down first.

* Check that the seals on fridge and freezer doors are working properly: they should be tight enough to hold a sheet of paper.

What causes air pollution?

Greenhouse gases aren't the only ones to pollute the Earth's atmosphere. Other gases cause problems too, among them chlorofluorocarbons – CFCs for short.

What's wrong with CFCs?

The Sun puts out harmful ultraviolet (UV) radiation, which is what gives us sunburn. Luckily, we're shielded from some of this by a layer of gas called ozone which lies around the Earth. But, for over 20 years, there has been a worrying hole in the ozone layer. In 2006, the hole was particularly big – nearly three times the size of the USA.

It's never been more important to slap on the suncream.

Back in the 1980s, scientists discovered the hole was being caused by CFCs. These were used in fridges, air conditioning systems and spray cans. CFCs have now been banned in most countries, but they stay in the atmosphere for up to 100 years. So it could take more than a lifetime for the hole to repair itself.

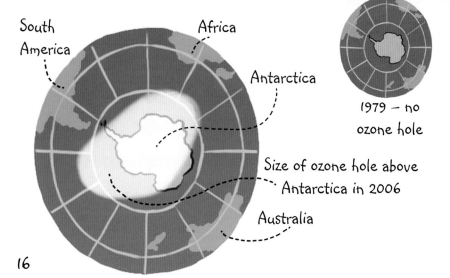

South America

Africa

Antarctica

1979 – no ozone hole

Size of ozone hole above Antarctica in 2006

Australia

Acid rain

Air pollution even affects the rain. Some of the gases produced by burning fossil fuels turn the rain acidic. This means it can damage plants and even buildings.

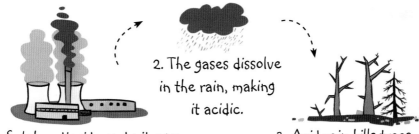

2. The gases dissolve in the rain, making it acidic.

1. Sulphur dioxide and nitrogen oxides rise into the air from power stations, factories and cars.

3. Acid rain kills trees, poisons river life, and wears away buildings.

What is smog?

Hundreds of thousands of people in the world die every year from breathing in smog – air that is clogged with pollution. Smog is caused by a mixture of smoke and waste gases, mostly pumped out from power stations, factories, cars and planes. It's worse on hot, still days, and people with breathing or heart problems are most at risk.

Many cities with the world's worst air pollution are in China and Russia. These countries have a lot of industry and their anti-pollution laws aren't always enforced.

Some big cities have a constant haze of smog hanging over them.

Getting around

A hundred years ago, it was quite rare for anyone to travel far from where they lived. But fast, modern ways of getting around mean that people are doing much more travelling – so much, in fact, that transport is now the fastest-growing source of CO_2 emissions and general air pollution.

The worst polluters

Planes are the most polluting kind of transport for each passenger mile travelled, with cars the next worst offenders. Car fumes contain a whole cocktail of dirt and gases, besides CO_2. In countries with heavy traffic, these fumes lead to even more deaths than traffic accidents. Some experts believe it isn't even healthy inside a car, because its plastics and fabrics pollute the air you're breathing.

Noise pollution causes stress for people living by busy roads or under flight paths.

What can governments do?

Some governments are trying to reduce plane travel by making it more expensive. And they're encouraging people to change the cars they drive by taxing big gas-guzzlers more than smaller, fuel-efficient ones. They can also improve public transport and make it easier for people to walk or cycle. Some cities now have trams, which produce no fumes and little noise.

What can I do?

* Take the train, if you can. Trains use only about a third of the energy of a plane for each mile travelled per passenger and cause only about a fifth of the pollution.

* Ferries are less polluting than planes per passenger mile.

* Buses and coaches do pollute, but because they carry lots of people at once, the amount of pollution per person is much less than if everyone went by car.

* Cycling causes no pollution at all, and is good exercise. You need to ride on safe cycle routes though, and wear a helmet and reflective clothing.

* Walking is a great option for short journeys. A two-mile walk takes about half an hour and counts as half the amount of daily exercise that doctors recommend.

* If you have to go to school by car, see if you can organize a shared school run with friends or neighbours so the car is full.
  It's short car journeys that cause the most intense pollution, because the heaviest emissions take place in the first two miles, while the engine is warming up.

Walking to school can be quicker than sitting in a traffic jam. And cars use more energy and cause more pollution in busy areas, because they are always stopping and starting.

A load of old rubbish

Until fairly recently, people used to put all their rubbish out for the bin men and then forget about it. But the mountains of rubbish we create are a big problem for the planet. At last, governments are working out ways to cut down on waste, and individuals are taking action too.

What's wrong with burying it?

Most household waste is taken to landfill sites, where it gets buried underground. This hides it away from view, but it leaves behind lots of problems.

One of the biggest worries is that some rubbish, such as batteries, hairspray and plastics, releases toxic, or poisonous, substances. These can escape into the air or leak into the soil and pollute water that runs underground. Some of this groundwater flows into rivers, harming wildlife. And human drinking water can get polluted too.

Squash your rubbish down so you don't need to use many bin liners.

Rubbish is very bulky, and more is being added to the heaps all the time, requiring new landfill sites. It won't rot away, but will hang around, possibly for ever, or at least for centuries. And food and garden waste in landfill produce methane, which contributes to global warming. The rubbish is taken to the landfill sites by road, so the journey causes yet more pollution. Last but not least, landfill sites smell.

Why not burn it?

Rubbish that isn't buried usually gets burned in incinerators. But this isn't a great solution either. Many incinerators pump fumes into the air that are harmful to the environment and to people, and they produce toxic ash which has to end up in landfill.

Bin your litter

Litter doesn't just look a mess. It can attract flies, mice and rats, and spread disease. And it can harm animals. Glass is dangerous as it can start fires if it is left in the hot sun.

For all these reasons, it's important always to take your rubbish with you. Wait until you find a bin to put it in, even if that means carrying it all the way home.

The pet poo problem

Dog and cat poo left in soil or sand can cause serious illness and even blindness if it gets in someone's mouth or eyes. Children are most at risk, when they are playing. So always clear up carefully after your dog, and train your cat to use a litter tray, so it's less likely to poo in other people's gardens.

Reduce, reuse, recycle

Over 60% of household waste can be recycled – broken down so that it can be made into something new. But it would be even better if everyone bought less stuff in the first place, and tried to get things repaired instead of binning them when they go wrong.

How do I reduce and reuse?

* Take things you no longer need to a charity shop, or join in a car boot sale. Try to shop at these places too.

* Use libraries and rental shops.

* Download music from the internet.

* Swap books, CDs, DVDs and computer games with friends.

* Refuse plastic bags in shops. Take your own bag or at least reuse old plastic ones. If you have a mountain of plastic bags at home, you could use the bags as bin liners or ask if your local charity shop or greengrocer can make use of them.

* Avoid disposables, such as plastic cups and single-use cameras. Wash empty mineral water bottles and reuse them.

* Use rechargeable, alkaline manganese batteries. Other types can leak toxic heavy metals into the soil in landfill sites.

* Use a stapleless stapler, or use and reuse paper clips.

* Ask your doctor, dentist or hairdresser if they would like your old magazines for their waiting rooms.

* Instead of buying a present for a relation, offer to help with jobs like gardening, car cleaning or decorating.

Why recycle?

Making a recycled drinks can only uses 5% of the energy of making one from scratch.

Recycling one glass bottle saves enough energy to power a TV for 1½ hours.

It's almost always less polluting, and cheaper, to recycle than to make things from scratch. Recycling cuts down on the materials, energy and water used in production.

How do I recycle?

Your local council should have a leaflet telling you what you can recycle, and whether they provide a doorstep collection, recycling banks, or bins, in car parks, or a big recycling dump. You need to follow the instructions for sorting your waste or it won't actually get recycled.

This symbol shows that a product can be recycled.

Buying recycled

Buy recycled stuff when you can. You'll find lots of recycled stationery and other paper products, and you can sometimes buy toiletries in returnable, refillable containers. But there are some wackier things around too, such as mouse mats made from old tyres and sleeping bags from shredded phone directories.

This symbol means that 50% of the product is made from recycled materials.

What can I recycle?

More things get added to the list of recyclables all the time, so it's always worth stopping to think if there's a better way to get rid of rubbish than just throwing it away. Check that your school is doing its bit, too. Here are some of the things you can recycle:

* Paper, glass, cans, and some, newer plastics. (If you're unsure, check by looking for a recycling symbol.) Wash out containers that have had food in them, but be careful not to cut yourself on cans. (There's more about recycling paper on page 41.)

* Biodegradable waste (see opposite page).

* If clothes are too old and shabby for the charity shop, put them in a textiles bank so they can be recycled.

* Mobile phones contain several highly toxic substances which can be released if left in landfills or incinerated. But 80% of a phone's materials can be recycled. Many phone shops, charity shops and even supermarkets run recycling schemes.

* You can recycle printer cartridges through various shops.

* Take old specs to an optician or charity shop that runs a recycling scheme. Your old ones might be just right for someone else. Some get sent to developing countries.

If you have recycling boxes, keep the lids firmly closed so animals can't injure themselves on your rubbish.

What is biodegradable?

Some waste is biodegradable, which means
that it rots away fairly quickly – that's if it isn't
starved of oxygen in a landfill site. Food scraps,
garden waste and paper are all biodegradable. Your
council may recycle this for you, but if you have a
garden you can do it yourself.

You can put it all in a compost bin or, if you
have a big garden, make a heap out of it
– well away from the house to avoid smells.
Then, leave it to rot down into a rich compost
– natural fertiliser – which you can spread on
your garden soil for super-healthy plants.

You can compost:

* Fruit and vegetable peelings
* Tea bags, tea leaves and coffee grounds
* Eggshells
* Cardboard (e.g. toilet roll tubes, cereal packets and egg boxes)
* Paper bags and paper towels, unless covered in food

* It helps if you tear up cardboard and paper into smallish pieces.
* Don't try to compost any meat, fish, dairy or cooked food at
   home. It will smell, attract mice and flies, and spread disease.

Some people even have a wormery. This is basically a
compost bin with worms – special composting worms that
you can buy. The worms munch through the rubbish, pass
it out their other end, and so turn it into compost faster.

Water pollution

Like all living things, we can't survive without water – it's not surprising as that's what we are mostly made of. Our drinking water needs to be clean to prevent us getting ill, but water can become polluted in lots of different ways.

What causes it?

Water gets polluted by chemical waste from factories, farms or landfill sites; by oil spills from ships; and even by litter.

In developing countries, the main cause of water pollution is human sewage (poo) and animal droppings. Millions of children's lives could be saved every year if they had safe drinking water and toilets, and if sewage drains didn't overflow during floods.

Dead zones

People used to think the sea was so vast that it could absorb any waste dumped in it. But there are now about 150 'dead zones' in the world's seas, where hardly anything can live.

The main cause is chemicals used in farming. They run off fields into streams and then into the sea. The chemicals start off a process which leaves the sea and its creatures starved of oxygen – so they die. One of the biggest dead zones is in the Gulf of Mexico. But it isn't too late. If pollution is reduced now, sea life may return.

Some creatures can escape from a dead zone to cleaner waters. Others, such as crabs, are too slow-moving.

How can I help keep water clean?

The really big problems of water pollution can only be tackled by governments, but everyone can do their bit to help keep rivers, lakes, seas and groundwater clean.

* Washing-up liquid, washing powder, and sink, bath and toilet cleaners all get flushed away and into rivers and seas. Try to use environmentally friendly brands, and see if you can get things clean with less.

* Don't put anything down the toilet apart from wee, poo and toilet paper. The sewage system can't cope with anything else, and other rubbish can get into rivers or onto beaches.

* Most of the oil that pollutes water comes from homes. Don't pour oil down the sink or outside drains. This goes for cooking oil and even the oil from your can of tuna or sardines. Instead, drain the oil into a plastic bottle, and put it in your rubbish for the bin men. (And yes, it's not good to throw away plastic but, on balance, causing oil pollution is probably even worse.) Let fat from cooked meat solidify, then wrap it in paper and put it in the bin.

   The oil from your family car should be taken to the recycling dump or a garage that runs a recycling scheme.

* Don't drop litter. It doesn't only pollute water but harms wildlife too.

Water shortage

Surely there's enough water for everyone?
Well, no – a third of the world's people don't
have enough. Many use less in a day for
drinking, cooking and washing than people in
developed countries do for a single loo flush.

In some countries, children don't have
time to go to school because they have to
trek to wells to fetch water for their families.

Not enough rain

Global warming is making water shortages worse. In
many places, including the traditionally rainy countries of
northern Europe, it now rains less than it used to. By 2025
two thirds of the world's people will probably live
in countries that are short of water.

How can I save water?

* Don't leave a tap running unnecessarily. It wastes 9 litres of
  water a minute. If you turn off the tap while you brush your
  teeth and turn it back on just for rinsing, you can save about
  80% of the water you'd otherwise use.
* Put a full plastic bottle or a brick in your toilet cistern. This
  will take up space normally filled by water, so you'll be using
  less every time you flush.
  * Have a shower instead of a bath. It should use half
    the amount of water or even less, especially if you
    turn the shower off while you soap yourself.

* Only put the washing machine or dishwasher on when there's a full load. Half-load settings use more than half the water of a full load.

* Put your clothes in the wash less often. If you fold them or hang them up so they don't look crumpled, you'll probably realize they aren't that dirty. If you have a garden, you can also freshen clothes up by hanging them out on the line for a while.

* Don't overfill the kettle. Just boil the amount of water you need.

* Don't run the tap to get the water really cold before you drink it. Fill a jug or bottle and chill it in the fridge for next time.

* Wash dishes and vegetables in a bowl, not under a running tap.

* Use washing-up water and bath water to water plants, as long as you haven't used strong detergent or bath oils. Best not to keep watering the same plants with this 'grey' water though – share it around.

* If you're giving someone a garden plant, buy a drought-resistant one – that's a plant that doesn't need much water, such as geranium or lavender.

* If you have a water butt in your garden, it will collect rainwater which you can use on plants.

* Wash your family car from a bucket. Automatic car washes and hosepipes use much more water.

* Be especially careful not to waste water if you are on holiday in a hot country.

* And finally, don't rush to flush – that's the loo after every wee. (It would be a good idea to discuss this with your family first!)

Chemical overload

Although most of the world's pollution comes from big industries, businesses and transport, there are some pollutants that are much closer to home.

In the home

There are tens of thousands of artificial chemicals in daily use – many, many more than when your grandparents were young. These chemicals are used in plastics, packaging, furniture, paint, cleaning products, toiletries and cosmetics. They are tested for safety, but no one can be sure how they will affect the environment – and people – over a long time.

Then: vinegar, water and elbow grease

Now: perfumed spray cleaner

In the human body

Household chemicals can be absorbed by the human body. Generally, you either breathe them in, or they get in through your skin. Even newborn babies' bodies already contain some. Some of these chemicals are called POCs (persistent organic compounds). They never disappear but just continue to build up during your lifetime.

How can I cut down on chemicals?

You can help keep the environment clean, and look after your own health, by using fewer of the products listed below – or at least try to choose alternatives with natural ingredients that are more environmentally friendly.

* Avoid perfumed cleaning products, polishes, washing-up liquid, biological detergents, fabric softeners, toilet and air fresheners and fly sprays. Not only do these get into you, they also get into the water and soil, when they go down the drain.

   Filthy sports kit might need biological detergent but most clothes come clean in the less harmful, non-biological sort.

* Cut down on toiletries and cosmetics, including deodorants, shower gels, hair products, body sprays, lip salves and make-up – especially if they are perfumed. Ask yourself if you really need them, or could use less. Read the long list of ingredients on the packaging and you may even want to cut down.

* Avoid food wrap, such as cling film. Instead, store food in washable containers and use greaseproof paper for sandwiches.

* Plastic bottles may leak chemicals into your drink. Bottles stamped PETE are considered the safest, but it may be best to drink from a glass or mug when you can.

* If you're decorating your bedroom, try to use VOC-free paint. VOCs (volatile organic compounds) are chemicals that pollute the air.

   Indoor plants can be useful as they help to absorb pollution.

Food for thought

In the richer parts of the world, many people eat too much to be healthy, while in other, poorer parts millions are starving. The world population is growing, so it's a major challenge to produce enough food and get it to the right places – all without damaging the planet.

Huge fields but only one crop

Monoculture, where one crop is grown over a large area, is big business, and can produce a huge amount of food efficiently and cheaply. But it has its problems. After a while, the soil tends to get worn out and produces less. And this kind of farming uses a lot of harmful artificial chemicals.

What's wrong with artificial chemicals?

Artificial pesticides are sprayed on crops to kill insects that damage them, herbicides are used to kill weeds, and fertilisers to help crops to grow. But these can all damage wildlife and pollute groundwater. The traces that remain on food may not be good for people either. No one can tell what the long-term effects will be.

There is less wildlife on farmland that is sprayed with chemicals and where hedges and trees have been cut down to make huge fields.

What is organic farming?

Organic farmers use methods that are as natural and non-polluting as possible. Organic pesticides, herbicides and fertilisers contain only a fraction of the harmful chemicals of non-organic ones. But organic farming needs more land to produce the same amount of food as non-organic. So organic farming alone could probably not feed the world.

Organic farms are home to many more birds and insects than non-organic ones.

What does GM mean?

GM (genetically modified) food comes from plants that have been changed – or modified – to grow in a different way. Scientists modify the plants' genes – the things that control the way a living thing looks and grows. They can do this to make food that doesn't rot as quickly, for example. But some people fear that genes from GM plants may spread to other plants and cause environmental damage.

Fishy issues

The world's fish stocks are in massive decline. Overfishing has meant that fish are caught before they have a chance to mate and reproduce. And modern fishing techniques can be wasteful. For every kilo of prawns caught, 12 kilos of other creatures are trapped in the nets and thrown back dead. Dolphins and turtles also get entangled in nets, and drown.

Food miles

The distance food travels from the field to your plate is measured in food miles. If you buy locally produced food, it avoids the pollution caused when food is transported long distances, sometimes by plane. It also means you get a chance to eat food that's in season where you live. It may be fresher and taste better too.

But it isn't as simple as that. Less electricity may be used to grow food abroad, for example if hothouses are not needed. So the total greenhouse gases produced may still add up to less, even with plane transport. And many developing countries depend for their living on the income they get from exporting food.

So what should I buy?

With so many issues to consider, it can be hard to know what to buy for the best. Here are some ideas that should help the planet, including the animals and people living on it.

* Buy organic. Organic farming is better for the environment, and trials are still being done to see if it is healthier to eat too. Organic meat won't have antibiotics in it.

* Buy free range meat and eggs. It's more likely the animals have been reared in natural conditions, with fresh air and space to move around.

* Look for fish approved by the Marine Stewardship Council. This means it has been caught in waters with adequate fish stocks and that other creatures haven't been harmed in the process.

* Buy 'dolphin-friendly tuna' – that's tuna caught with nets that limit harm to dolphins.

* Watch out for new labels showing how much greenhouse gas has been created by producing and transporting a food.

* Cut down on food miles by shopping near your home if you can, instead of driving a long way to buy your food.

* Look for Fairtrade coffee, tea, chocolate and bananas. Fairtrade means that farmers and workers in developing countries get a fairer share of the money you've paid. And they are not allowed to use harmful chemicals.

* Buy products with the least packaging. There may be less at a local greengrocer's, butcher's or farmers' market. In some supermarkets you can now buy tubes of food like tomato purée straight from display holders instead of in individual boxes that you throw away. About 15% of what you pay for a ready meal goes on packaging.

* Don't take mini-packs or individually wrapped snacks like biscuits in your lunchbox. Instead, open bigger packs, wrap what you need in biodegradable greaseproof paper, and store the rest in an airtight container.

* Don't waste food. Keep leftovers in the fridge or freezer for another time.

Wildlife in danger

Biologists estimate that there are at least 5 million, and perhaps as many as 30 million, different species, or types, of plants and animals on the planet. But many of them – at least 16,000 – are at risk of dying out. It's natural for species to become extinct sometimes, but now it's happening on a large scale, and mainly because of people's activities.

Golden toads were declared extinct in 2004. Climate change and pollution were probably responsible.

What's biodiversity?

Biodiversity is the richness and variety of life on Earth. Many people believe that humans have no right to put other species in danger. And if we don't respect wildlife, life becomes poorer for us too.

All living things, including people, are linked together in a complex web of survival, and the tiniest creatures can be as important as the large ones. For example, some bacteria make water safer to drink. They break down traces of toxic chemicals that have got into it.

What's more, research has shown that it is good for people's mental health and physical fitness to spend time in natural environments.

It's important to keep to paths in the countryside, to avoid causing damage.

What are the major threats?

The main danger to wildlife comes from human activities that destroy its natural homes, or habitats. This happens when land is cleared for farming, mining or building. Sumatran rabbits, in Indonesia, are under threat because their forest habitat is being destroyed for farming.

Some animals are hunted, and plants are harvested, to the point where they are in danger of dying out.

Tigers are endangered partly because they are hunted illegally for their fur and for their body parts which are used in medicines in China.

Sometimes species are threatened when people introduce a new, non-native species into their habitat. The new species may compete with them for food or even kill them.

Ships brought rats, cats and stoats to New Zealand. They ate the eggs of ground-nesting birds called kakapos, driving them to the edge of extinction.

Both land and sea habitats are damaged by pollution, for example by pesticides or by oil spills from tankers. Global warming is also a problem.

Now that the ice is melting in the Arctic, polar bears' hunting grounds are dwindling and they are going hungry.

What's special about coral reefs?

Coral reefs are hugely biodiverse as they are home to more than a quarter of all sea species. The reefs develop in warm, tropical waters, but now global warming is making the sea so warm that they are dying. They are also threatened by fishing, pollution and tourists.

Litter alert

Litter is a real danger to animals, as they can mistake it for food or get tangled up in it. A lot of street litter gets swept down drains and often ends up in the sea.

Turtles sometimes mistake plastic bags for jellyfish, one of their favourite foods. But swallowing the bags can kill them.

How does conservation help?

There are more and more conservation projects that are working successfully to save endangered species. Numbers of some threatened animals and plants are even on the increase again now.

Mauritius kestrels are less at risk than they were, thanks to projects which protected their nest sites.

How can I help?

* Support conservation projects. You can even adopt or sponsor an animal. The money you give either pays for its care or goes to help protect the species in general.

* Never drop litter, even if it's biodegradable. Even an apple core or banana skin can make some animals ill.

* Feed the birds in your garden. You need to be sure of how to do this without harming them, though. See page 47 for where to find a website to help you do this.

* If you don't have a garden, you could put plants in window boxes or on your balcony to attract insects such as butterflies.

* Don't pick wild flowers. In many places it is illegal anyway. The entire plant may die, and the flowers can't make seeds.

* Don't take pebbles or rocks from the beach. They help to hold the sand in place and there may be creatures living underneath.

* Don't buy shells or sea 'curios'. They will have been captured alive and the animals removed from inside the shells.

* Don't buy foil or helium balloons. Foil isn't biodegradable and helium is a valuable gas which could run out one day. Instead, buy latex balloons, which biodegrade. And don't let any balloons drift away. They can all be a menace to wildlife, and even latex ones take several months to degrade.

* See pages 34-35 for some food ideas that can help prevent damage to animals.

39

Disappearing forests

Natural forests are being destroyed very quickly. Every single minute, an area of forest the size of 35 football pitches disappears. A lot of it is deliberately burned to clear the land for farming. In other places, the trees are felled to provide wood for buildings and furniture.

Why does it matter?

Forests are known as carbon sinks, because they store CO_2. But when they are burned, the CO_2 is released. Forest-burning now accounts for as much as one fifth of all the CO_2 emissions caused by human activity.

If you can, plant shrubs or trees in your garden. They help to absorb and store CO_2 as well as providing shelter for birds and other wildlife.

Some natural forests, especially rainforests, are hugely biodiverse. Their destruction is threatening many species with extinction.

SAVE OUR HOME!

Spotted-tailed quolls are at risk from a time when parts of the Australian rainforest were being destroyed.

Forest plants can be useful. They provide food such as fruit and nuts, and even some medicines. Trees can also help to prevent floods by anchoring the soil with their roots.

What about trees and paper?

Paper generally comes from trees in managed plantations, so that new trees are planted to replace those that are felled. But plantations are much less rich in plant and animal life than natural forests.

And we throw away mountains of paper – even more paper than food waste, at least in Europe and the USA. It makes sense to reduce the amount we use, as well as to recycle.

I tonne of recycled paper saves 30,000 litres of water.

What can I do?

* Recycle paper.
* Write, print and photocopy on both sides of your paper.
* Reuse envelopes – you can stick labels over the old address.
* Buy recycled stationery, tissues, toilet and kitchen rolls, and animal bedding.
* Make gift tags from old cards.
* Buy wood and paper that is labelled as coming from a sustainable source. This book, for example, is printed on paper approved by the Forest Stewardship Council.
* Don't use kitchen roll or tissues to mop up spills. Use a cloth you can wash out and reuse instead.
* Use a chalkboard, instead of paper, for writing messages at home.

PUT OUT RECYCLING

Footprints on the planet

Most scientists agree that climate change is the biggest problem facing the planet, and so reducing greenhouse gases is the most important challenge of all. Many emissions come from homes – over a quarter of the UK's total, for example. Soon, everyone is going to have to think about their carbon footprint.

What is a carbon footprint?

A carbon footprint is the amount of CO_2 and other greenhouse gases that an individual, a business or a country produces. There are websites where you can calculate your own family's footprint, from the amount of energy you use in your home, to the way you get around, and even the food you eat. See page 47 for how to find a website to help you do this.

Whose footprints are biggest?

Roughly three quarters of the world's greenhouse gases are produced by only a quarter of the world's population – that's people in the richer countries. So it's up to richer countries to lead the way in cutting down. Many people in developing countries would like to enjoy the lifestyles that those in developed countries have had for some time, so it isn't fair to expect them to cut back before developed countries do.

USA

Pakistan   Carbon footprints
per person

Making footprints smaller

It probably won't be enough to rely on people saving energy voluntarily, so in the future everyone may be given a carbon quota, or allowance, by their government. If you don't want to use it all, you could sell off some of it. And if, for example, you want to make long plane journeys, which will produce lots of greenhouse gases, you could buy an increased quota.

Already, some businesses and individuals are trying to compensate for their emissions by putting money into green projects, such as renewable energy or rainforest restoration. This is called carbon offsetting. It is better than nothing, but the only real solution still has to be: cut down.

One carbon offset scheme provides more efficient stoves for developing countries.

New stoves use less wood for fuel and cut down on unhealthy smoke.

Can science solve the problem?

Scientists have worked out a way of capturing CO_2 and storing it, so that it can't get into the atmosphere and cause damage. They can pump it into rocks or inject it deep into the seabed. But it is expensive to do this and they need to be sure it won't leak out in the future.

So, despite these new possibilities, it's still vitally important that we move away from carbon-producing fuels and towards more green, renewable alternatives.

Green living

So what will it be like if we start living a green life? Will it be dull, or might it even be better? Some people are already living more sustainably, in specially designed eco-homes, and believe it has improved their quality of life. Here are some of the aims of green living.

You try to be carbon neutral – to produce no, or very little, CO_2. Some renewable energy is generated on site, and the rest comes from green-energy suppliers. You offset your carbon emissions.

Your appliances are energy-efficient and all lighting is low-energy.

Solar roof panels provide your hot water and some electricity.

Houses are built from local natural materials, such as wood from a sustainable source, and recycled materials.

Rainwater is collected on the roof and used for the washing machine, flushing the toilet and watering the garden.

A dual-flush toilet means you use less water for wee, more for poo.

Your family belongs to a car club and you borrow a car when you need to.

You grow your own vegetables.

You go to school on the walking bus – the 'driver' comes round and picks you up from your house.

Signs of success

If most of what you hear about the planet seems gloomy, it helps to know that some things are improving.

* Protected areas, such as wildlife reserves, now cover 10% of the Earth's land – a big achievement for conservationists.

* Wildlife is returning to water that has been cleaned up. The river Dove in England used to be too polluted for salmon to survive there. Now they are back.

* Many countries in the developed world have air pollution laws.

* Some big cities have traffic-free centres, or congestion zones that you have to pay to take your car into.

* Recycling rates are improving. Austria and the Netherlands, for example, recycle over 60% of their rubbish.

* People have become aware that disposable plastic bags harm the environment. In some places you are no longer given them free at shop checkouts. Either you have to buy them or they are not available at all.

* If you have an ethical bank account, the bank promises it will not invest your money in ways that harm people or the planet.

* Campaigning can work. 'Save the whale' campaigns have made whaling unacceptable in most countries. And governments are at last trying to tackle climate change, thanks to campaigners.

If everyone lived like people in developed countries, it would take at least three planets to provide us with all the resources we need, such as water, oil or trees. We don't have three planets but we do have one. It can support us all – if we take better care of it.

Glossary

climate – typical weather conditions in a particular place.

conservation – protecting and maintaining environments including the plants, animals and buildings that are part of them.

deforestation – reducing or destroying forests by cutting down or burning trees.

desertification – the spread of desert conditions into areas that weren't previously desert.

developing country – a country where, in general, many people rely on farming, advanced technology is limited and wages are low.

ecological – causing as little damage to the environment as possible, or positively benefiting it.

ecological footprint – the amount of damage a person, family, business or country does to the environment. This is based on the area of land and sea needed to provide them with all the resources they use – food, energy, clothes, transport etc – and to absorb their waste.

ecosystem – a large area with a similar climate and all the living things in the area.

environment – surroundings, including the landscape, air and living things.

extinct species – a type of plant or animal that has died out.

fuel – material that can be burned to provide heat or power.

global warming – a rise in average temperatures around the world.

green – causing as little damage to the environment as possible, or positively benefiting it.

ozone – a gas which forms a protective layer around the Earth. Close to the ground, ozone is produced by vehicle exhaust fumes combined with sunlight, and is harmful to people's health.

pollution – harmful waste or dirt which builds up faster than it can be broken down.

sustainable – using only the amount of the planet's resources that is possible without damaging it for future generations.

Internet links

For links to websites where you can find out more about saving the planet, go to the Usborne Quicklinks Website at www.usborne-quicklinks.com and type the keywords: save the planet. The recommended websites are regularly reviewed and updated but, please note, Usborne Publishing is not responsible for the content of websites other than its own. We advise you to read the internet safety guidelines at Usborne Quicklinks before you start.

Index

Photographic manipulation by Catherine-Anne MacKinnon. Additional designs by Vicky Arrowsmith.

First published in 2008 by Usborne Publishing Ltd, Usborne House, 83-85 Saffron Hill, London EC1N 8RT,
England. www.usborne.com Copyright © 2008 Usborne Publishing Ltd. The name Usborne and the
devices 💡 🐝 are Trade Marks of Usborne Publishing Ltd. All rights reserved. No part of this publication
may be reproduced, stored in a retrieval system or transmitted in any form or by any means, electronic,
mechanical, photocopying, recording or otherwise, without the prior permission of the publisher.
Printed in China.